Praise for In Between the Sheets/Max Melvin

It has been my privilege to observe the life and ministry of Pastor Max Melvin over the past two decades. In that time, this servant of God has hungered and thirsted after God himself while ministering to God's people. In dealing with his family, church, and community, he has sought to glorify his Savior, the Lord Jesus Christ.

The Bible says, "A nation falls through a lack of guidance, but victory comes through the counsel of many (Psalm 11:14)." For those seeking a compact and concise book on marriage counseling, Marriage in Between the Sheets by Pastor Max Melvin is a must! -Rev. Dr. Gordon H. Young, Pastor, New Revelation Missionary Baptist Church, Baltimore, Maryland

With profound gratitude, I would like to thank Pastor Max Melvin for his leadership, guidance, support, and most importantly his love for my family. Words can't express my thankfulness for his presence in our lives. His continual sacrifice and willingness to provide his time aligns with his teachings. Those teachings guided me personally to understand the role of the man in a family with correlation to scriptures. Thank you for being that voice in my head as the daily challenges arise. "Love equals total responsibility" will live with me forever. I am so elated to see you finally share your gift with the world. God will lead you to new heights beyond your imagination and use you as a vehicle to bless others. For generations to come, your legacy will live on through your literature. Let's celebrate as you elevate! - Derek Tinsley, Client

I have known Pastor Melvin for over 40 years. We have been best friends since the beginning and I think of him as a brother. I have witnessed his evolution from a young, scrappy football player to a charismatic pastor and leader. Pastor Melvin has always been charismatic, witty, and wise. I knew he was destined for great things.

When he informed me that he wanted to become a minister, I told him if he did, then when I got married I wanted him to preside over my ceremony. We both held up our end of the bargain and 25 years later, we are still best friends, and I am still married. Pastor Melvin has counseled us along the way. Pastor Melvin has developed into a world-class counselor. His vast knowledge base makes him able to counsel people and couples from all walks of life. - Anthony A. Humphries, Client

I have known Max for over 40 years. I was his teacher and football coach at Oxon Hill Senior High School, and now I'm his friend. Max has grown to be a remarkable man. He's a devoted husband to his wife Sheila, a loving father to his daughter, Shannon, and committed Pastor of New Beginnings Christian Center. Max always had a thirst to engage me and others in conversations that challenged us to think deeply about scripture. He would research what the scriptures were saying, and then discuss what he learned with us. I knew Max's desire to learn more about the Lord would lead him into ministry. I truly believe Max has a calling from the Lord. Max leads by example and what you see on Sundays in the pulpit is who he is. I am truly blessed to know Max and when I have occasion to visit New Beginnings Christian Center, I know he'll provide my wife and I with a good word from the Lord. - Michael A Pearson, Sr., President/CEO, AFC Scholarship Foundation, Inc.

Marriage in Between the Sheets

MAX T. MELVIN

Marriage in Between the Sheets

ISBN: 978-1-946909-04-6 (Print)
978-1-946909-05-3 (eBook)

Cover Design by Norbert Elnar, Masterpiece Kingdom Brands
Interior Design by Erica D. Welch, By Her Shelf Media

Printed in the U.S.A.

DEDICATION

This book is dedicated to my wife, Sheila Melvin. It is because of you that this message of marriage will bring joy and love to so many others. You have been an instrument in the hands of God to help me fulfill my life's purpose. Thank you for believing in every vision the Lord has given me. Without your help, my life would be unfulfilled. You are my best friend, my companion, my lover, and the most incredible woman in this world to me. I love you more than any words could ever express!

Contents

Foreword

Over the past 40 years, Pastor Max T. Melvin has been a close friend, mentor, brother, and excellent counselor and pastor. I recall Pastor Melvin ecouraging me to get a real relationship with Jesus Christ in my early twenties. There were times he would lovingly chastise me, and there were many times we laughed together.

Pastor Melvin and I attended Washington Saturday College together in our early thirties. We grew tremendously in the word of God there. We both can recall one of our instructors demanding that when we counsel God's people, we do so nouthetically-- based on the word of God. I can personally attest to the changed lives of many people I've known personally who were counseled by Pastor Melvin. Pastor Melvin is a no-nonsense pastor who takes the word of God seriously.

Pastor Melvin comes from humble beginnings. I can appreciate his open, honest, and down to earth approach to dealing with people. He is the kind of person who can discern when you're being honest and transparent and when you're not.

Pastor Melvin is also a true family man. He always places his family first right after God. When I think of our many years of friendship, I'm thankful to God for placing him in my life and I know he reciprocates the same feelings.

I remember about twenty years ago when Pastor Melvin was starting his new church. He began humbly, transporting all his church's belongings in a small pick-up truck each Sunday. But God rewards faithfulness, and now he is pastor over many souls with an established church facility.

As I think about where God has brought Pastor Melvin from and where He's taking him, I am amazed by his journey! It has been my privilege and honor to be a part of such a great move of God. I'm more than excited about this excellent book Pastor Melvin has written to help families build and maintain marriages. This book will bless anyone with a willing heart, open mind, and convicted spirit to grow in the things of God. I believe this book is just the beginning for my dear friend Pastor Max Melvin. I believe God has greater in store for him and his family.

Lastly, I want to say that I am so proud of my friend and brother. He has my full support and endorsement of this great work God placed in his hands and heart to produce. Do not miss your blessing! As you read, study, and follow these excellent, godly principles, watch the hand of the Lord transform your life forever!

Sincerely,

Minister Mark E. Osborne (In His service)

Introduction

Have you ever needed some important information? I'm talking about information that could change your life for the better. Often when we are seeking information, we search for it in all the wrong places. We go to friends, family, and other outside sources. This often yields partial assistance or no assistance at all.

If your car breaks down, would you seek assistance from a grocery store? Of course not! You would go to the manufacturer of the car. Why? Because they would be the ones with all the information. Well, I'm here to guide you to a better understanding of where your help comes from, specifically as it relates to marriage.

Everything God created in the universe was made with a successful vision and plan in mind. God has a plan for everything, including you, your spouse, and your marriage. Proverbs 19:21 tells us "Many are the plans in a person's heart, but it is the Lord's purpose that prevails."

If you have a situation in your marriage that requires assistance, or you need information, you should go to the creator of marriage...GOD. You must read the manual the Creator of the institution gave you.

God's plan for the institution of marriage is located in between the sheets of the Bible. From Genesis to Revelation, God has laid out His master plan for making great marriages work. The bible is where you will find the answers you've been searching for.

For over thirty years, with the help of the Holy Spirit, I've helped couples build and renew their marriages through the Word of God. My hope is that by studying God's point of view, you will receive divine revelations and godly understanding for your marriage.

This book is designed to give you the tools and insight you need to begin building a long and loving marriage. Get ready to climb in between the sheets of God's word and allow the Almighty Designer and Originator of the institution to help you and your spouse fulfill the plan He has for your marriage.

CHAPTER ONE

Counting the Cost of A Successful Marriage

It's been said that after your faith in God, marriage will be the most important decision you will make in your life. The person you choose to spend your life with will determine whether or not you will be happy or sad, poor or well off, successful or unsuccessful. Your choice in a marriage partner is vitally important.

Notice I said "your choice." God doesn't choose our partners. God presents people, but we have to make the choice. From the beginning of time, God only presented people.

He never makes choices for us. In Genesis 2:21-25, God created the woman from the rib which He had taken from man, then He brought her to the man. If you are going to have the partner of your dreams, you will have to make the right choice based on who crosses your path.

> And Adam said, "this is now bone of my bones and flesh of my flesh: She shall be called Woman because she was taken out of man." - Genesis 2:23

Adam made the decision to have the woman the Lord God had created. Adam, not God, said the woman was bone of his bones and flesh of his flesh. Adam chose her and took responsibility for her.

The reason God doesn't choose our partners is because if the relationship failed, we would blame Him. In Genesis 3:12, when Adam failed in the garden, the man said, "the woman you gave to be with me, she gave me of the tree and I did eat." It's part of our fallen nature to blame others for what is our responsibility. Adam took the responsibility in Genesis 2:21-25. He said she was taken out of man, so I am responsible for her.

THE ORIGINAL MODEL

> So God created mankind in his own image, in the image of God he created them; male and female he created them.
> - Genesis 1:27

God created a male and a female. But He said, "a man shall leave his mother and father and cleave to his wife and the two shall become one flesh" (Genesis 2:24).

Every male isn't a man but every man is a male.

> Then the Lord God formed a man from the dust of the ground and breathed into his nostrils the breath of life, and the man

> became a living being. - Genesis 2:7

This is the making of a MAN. Every man needs God to breathe into him the breath of life called the Holy Spirit so he can begin to live. Secondly, in verse eight, the Lord God placed the man in the garden of Eden with Himself.

The first thing a man needs before he gets a wife is a relationship with God.

> Submit to God and be at peace with him; in this way prosperity will come to you. Accept instruction from his mouth and lay up his words in your heart. If you return to the Almighty, you will be restored. - Job 22:21-23

Job 22:27 says, "You will pray to him, and he will hear you, and you will fulfill your vows." Man needs a relationship with God so the Lord can help him fulfill his promises to his wife and his vows to God.

Secondly, a man needs a job before he gets a wife.

> The Lord God took the man and put him in the garden of Eden to work it and take care of it. Genesis 2:15

The Lord God, in His omniscient wisdom, gave the man a job before He gave the man a wife. One of the greatest causes of divorce is finances. If a man isn't working, he cannot be the provider for his family. This can lead to low self-esteem, anger, depression, and feeling less than a man. It also puts unjust pressure on the family, especially the wife, which could leave her feeling overwhelmed and frustrated.

> Better to live on a corner of the roof than share a house with a quarrelsome wife. - Proverbs 21:9

> Better to live in a desert than with a quarrelsome and nagging wife. - Proverbs 21:19

If a man doesn't have a job for a long period of time, it can drive his wife crazy. God said, "it's better to live in the desert." Do you know what exists in the desert? Snakes that bite, scorpions that sting, and heat that can kill you from dehydration. God said it's better to live out there than in a house with a nagging wife. Because she is going to nag you until you get a JOB.

A man's job allows him to find fulfillment, feel important, and it gives him satisfaction. In fact, a man's job will give him more satisfaction than his wife. This is why it's God, not Adam, who says "It is not good for the Man to be alone. I will make a suitable helper for him" (Genesis 2:18). Adam was so busy that God told him he needed a wife. The man should be so preoccupied with his purpose that God has to tell him "you need a helper." A man's job also tells him why he exists and helps him define his purpose, his reason for living.

Sisters, this should not make you feel less important or secondary. When he finds you, he needs to be doing something so you can fulfill your God-created purpose. The last thing a woman needs in her life is a man who makes her feel like she has no reason to exist.

A woman is born ready to help. She comes prepackaged with all kinds of gifts to help a man fulfill his purpose if he will allow her. She has insight, intelligence, intuition, sensitivity to wisdom, incubation, gifts, power, anointing, and knowledge. These are all given to her to help the man. Man, don't fight against her. Allow her to work with you to carry out God's plans for your life. Then the scriptures can be fulfilled in your life:

> Again, truly I tell you that if two of you on earth agree about anything they ask for, it will be done for them by my Father in heaven. For where two or three gather in my name, there am I with them. - Matthew 18:19-20 NIV

The Bible also says,

> Two are better than one, because they have a good return for their labor: If either of them falls down, one can help the other

> up. But pity anyone who falls and has no one to help them up. Also, if two lie down together, they will keep warm. But how can one keep warm alone? Though one may be overpowered, two can defend themselves. A cord of three strands is not quickly broken. - Ecclesiastes 4:9-12 NIV

Now we can clearly see God's plan for His creation in action: the man, knowing his purpose (job), and allowing his wife (his helper) to help him, fulfilling God's assignment with the help of the Almighty God.

Lastly, a man needs God's word. David said, "thy word is a lamp unto my feet and a light into my path" (Psalm 119:105 KJV).

If we're going to make it through this dark world, we need the word of God to shine brightly in our lives. There are so many pitfalls and challenges that we can encounter in life, especially in marriage. Life just happens, period. You will not be able to avoid problems in your marriage. They are guaranteed to come. God knew you would have marital problems. He said those who marry will face many troubles in this life.

This is why the man needs God's word. The answers to many of the problems he will face are found in the Word of God. The Word will teach him how to love his wife and children. The Word will teach him what his role is as a husband (Head), and what that truly means.

> Husbands, love your wives, just as Christ loved the church and gave himself up for her to make her holy, cleansing her by the washing with the water through the word. Ephesians 5:25-26 NIV

If a man doesn't have the word, he cannot possibly know how to please his wife. He has to get the manufacturer's instructions on how she was created to function. She is so well put together by God. She is sophisticated, complicated, and simply amazing.

When God created Eve, he put Adam to sleep. He said in essence, "Adam, go to bed because this project I'm about to take on is going to take a while." So, if a man is going to understand his wife, he needs to get instructions from the manufacturer, who is God.

The Apostle Paul told his young protégé Timothy to "study to shew thyself approved unto God, a workman that needeth not to be ashamed, rightly dividing the word of truth" (2 Timothy 2:15).

Every man needs to study the word to find out how to live peacefully with his wife. Your knowledge of the word will determine whether or not your marriage will have a chance for success. Hosea reminds us, "my people are destroyed for lack of knowledge: because thou have rejected knowledge, I will also reject thee, that thou shalt be no priest to me: seeing thou hast forgotten the law of thou God, I will also forget thy children" (Hosea 4:6 KJV).

This scripture should scare the ignorance out of you. Because this is how I believe generational curses are passed down. If the son does not see the father carry out his role as a man and a husband, then he has to look elsewhere or try to figure it out on his own. This is where I believe the destruction of families begins. God said, "I will reject you and your children." I don't believe it's God rejecting us, but we have rejected the knowledge of God's word. For God has said, "I will never leave you nor will I forsake you " (Hebrews 13:5b).

When we go away from God's word, then we leave Him. He doesn't leave us. Men, put yourselves under the word so the word can brighten up your marriage and your family.

HOW DO WE MAKE THE RIGHT CHOICE?

The Lord knows how important the decision of choosing a good partner is to us. He equips us with the necessary resources to make the right choice. He gives us wisdom.

The book of Proverbs was written by King Solomon, one of the wisest men to have ever lived. Solomon also had 700 wives and 300 concubines. He should know a little about women and what it takes to live with them. In Proverbs 2, Solomon encourages us to incline our ears to wisdom and our hearts to understanding (v. 2). We must seek after wisdom and search after her as hidden treasures (v. 4). Why?

The Lord gives wisdom; out of His mouth comes knowledge and understanding. He lays up sound wisdom for the righteous (v. 6-7). When wisdom enters into our heart, knowledge is pleasant unto our souls (v. 10).

Proverbs 4:5-7 says,

> Get wisdom, get understanding: forget it not; neither decline from the words of my mouth. Forsake her not, and she shall preserve you: love her and she shall keep you. Wisdom is the principal thing; therefore get wisdom: and with all of your getting get understanding.

God gives us the wisdom to make the right choice. James 1:5 says, "if any of you lack wisdom, let him ask of God, that giveth to all men liberally."

The decision to marry someone must be carefully thought out. Remember, this is one of the most important decisions of your life. Proverbs 14:29 teaches us that "he that is hasty of spirit exalteth folly."

Luke 14:28 says we must first count the cost of marriage. Luke gives us some basic instructions on how to systematically go about the marriage process.

The first thing Doctor Luke tells us to do is to sit down. Marriage shouldn't be a quick decision. We need to get into God's Word and His presence. Let us find out what God has to say about the institution He created. He's the Maker of marriage and it originated from Him. We should ask ourselves some questions. "Why do 50% of all marriages fail?" "How can I be in the 50% that succeed?" "Who were my examples of marriage?" "Were they successful or not?"

Next, Luke asks us to count the cost. Estimate, use your imagination, project, predict, plan. People who plan have a better chance of success. Whether your marriage fails or succeeds depends on the plans you have or don't have. Proverbs 16:1 says, "To humans belong the plans of the heart, but from the Lord comes the proper answer of the tongue" (NIV).

Planning is our responsibility. We must be responsible for controlling time and chance in our lives. Proverbs 16:3 says, "Commit to the Lord whatever you do, and He will establish your plans." Verse 4 says, "The Lord works out everything to its proper end." That includes your marriage.

Lastly, we must see if we have what it takes to finish the race. Marriage is a marathon, not a sprint. The marathon is a 26.2-mile race. It's not for everyone. Neither is marriage. The discipline and the demand it takes to run a marathon is almost unbearable. It will ask everything of you and then some. So it is with marriage. There's a price to be paid if we are going to be successful at marriage. We make the vows at the wedding ceremony: "For better or worse," "for richer or poorer," "in sickness or health," "'til death do us part."

If we stay married long enough, there's a good chance we will experience all the vows we've made. Like the marathon runner, let us prepare ourselves for the race so we can finish strong.

CHAPTER TWO

Love, the Glue that Keeps Us Together

When couples come into my office and tell me they want to get married, the first question I ask them is "Why are you getting married?" Over the years, I've gotten some pretty remarkable answers, such as "she is so pretty." "He is so fine." "I feel like this is my soul mate." "We look good together." "They complete me."

All of these answers sound good, but the truth is they won't keep a marriage together. Your marriage will face many ups, downs, turnarounds, and changes over the years. There may be times when you don't like what the other person is doing or saying in the relationship. They might be going through a rough season in their lives when they may not like themselves, let alone you. How will you survive the for better or worse season?

When all else fails, love should be the glue keeping you together.

Let me give you my definition of love. Love is not just a feeling or an emotion that we sometimes have.

Love is a responsibility. We have a responsibility to take care of one another, take care of one another's needs, and help to fulfill one another's purposes on this Earth. These are only a few of the reasons God has brought us together.

> If I speak in the tongues of men or of angels, but do not have love, I am only a resounding gong or a clanging cymbal. If I have the gift of prophecy and fathom all mysteries and all knowledge, and if I have a faith that can move mountains, but do not have love, I am nothing. If I give all I possess to the poor and give over my body to hardship that I may boast, but do not have love, I gain nothing. Love is patient, love is kind. It does not envy, it does not boast, it is not proud. It does not dishonor others, it is not self-seeking, it is not easily angered, it keeps no record of wrongs. Love does not delight in evil but rejoices with the truth. It always protects, always trusts, always hopes, always perseveres. ***LOVE NEVER FAILS.*** But where there are prophecies, they will cease; where there are tongues, they will be stilled; where there is knowledge, it will pass away. - 1 Corinthians 13:1-8 (emphasis added)

Out of all the things we can bring to a marriage --money, material things, knowledge, experience, wisdom, etc.-- LOVE has to be the glue that keeps us together. Why? Because love never fails.

> A cord of three strands is not quickly broken. - Ecclesiastes 3:12b

Often in a counseling session, I tell the man, "For your marriage to really work, you and your wife must have a threesome." Initially, the man's eyes light up. But before he can get too happy, I tell him the third partner must be God. Love will keep us when we cannot keep ourselves.

> Dear friends, let us love one another, for love comes from God. Everyone who loves has been born of God and knows God. Whosoever does not love does not know God, because ***GOD IS LOVE.*** - 1 John 4:7 (emphasis added)

God and Love are one and the same. All marriages need the love of God to survive.

CHAPTER THREE

Sex, Love & Releasing the Load

As you read this book, you will realize great marriages base their origin off much more than what goes on "in between the sheets." Marriage has more to do with life outside of the bed than inside it. We spend more time outside of the bedroom than we do inside of it, and when we are inside of it, we probably do more sleeping than having sex. So, what do we do when we realize there is more to marriage than what we do between the sheets?

I'm not saying sex doesn't play a vital role in the life of the marriage. However, great sex doesn't start in the bed. It starts with what you do before you get there.

One of the greatest lovers ever to exist is a man God inconspicuously placed in the middle of the Bible. He wrote a book called The Song of Solomon, a book of poetry talking about his encounters with his 700 wives and more than 300 concubines.

In studying the poetry of Solomon, I found the secret to what made him such a great lover. Listen to the words of a man who had to know how to please his wives. Solomon didn't start in between the sheets, even though he might have ended up there. Listen to him romance his wife like a conductor directs a symphony:

> Like a lily among thorns is my darling among the young women. Like an apple tree among the trees of the forest is my beloved among the young men. I delight to sit in his shade, and his fruit is sweet to my taste. Let him lead me to the banquet hall, and let his banner over me be love. Strengthen me with raisins, refresh me with apples, for I am faint with love. His left arm is under my head, and his right arm embraces me. Daughters of Jerusalem, I charge you by the gazelles and by the does of the field: Do not arouse or awaken love until it so desires.
> -Song of Solomon 2:2-8

Solomon didn't start in the bedroom, but in the *mind* of his wife. She sees herself as the object of his affection. He makes her feel like she is the most important woman in Jerusalem. With elegance and gracefulness, he carefully cultivates her mind. Then, like a surgeon operating on his patient, Solomon begins to pay attention to the details of his wife:

> How beautiful you are, my darling! Oh, how beautiful! Your eyes behind your veil are doves. Your hair is like a flock of goats descending from the hills of Gilead. Your

> teeth are like a flock of sheep just shorn, coming up from the washing. Each has its twin; not one of them is alone. Your lips are like a scarlet ribbon; your mouth is lovely. Your temples behind your veil are like the halves of a pomegranate. Your neck is like the tower of David, built with courses of stone; on it hang a thousand shields, all of them shields of warriors. Your breasts are like two fawns, like twin fawns of a gazelle that browse among the lilies. Until the day breaks and the shadows flee, I will go to the mountain of myrrh and to the hill of incense. You are altogether beautiful, my darling; there is no flaw in you. Song of Songs 4:1-7

Solomon pays attention to every aspect of his wife's body. He pays attention to her needs over his needs. Because true love will always ask the question, "what can I do for you?" True love always gives more than it takes. Solomon is giving her what every woman desires: to be seen and heard. Men, are you listening??!!!! She wants to be seen above your job, career, and toys (because boys like to play with their toys).

Solomon tells his wife how beautiful she is to him. He starts with her hair. Brothers, do you know how much it costs for your wife to keep her hair looking good for you? You should try paying for it about a year, then you would truly appreciate what it takes to keep her looking attractive for you. Every time my wife comes home from the hairdresser, I'm always the first to tell her how beautiful her hair looks. Compliment her on how good she looks for you.

But Solomon didn't stop with her hair. He looked into her eyes. It has been said that the eyes are the windows to the soul. The soul is the mind, will, emotion, intellect. He looked into her eyes to see how she was feeling. He looked to see what was going on with her as a person. He cared about her. He just didn't want to know who she was on the outside but more importantly who she was on the inside. He made love to her mind. Her thoughts were important to him. I can hear him say in his Barry White voice "what are you thinking girl? I want to know what's on your mind. Tell me your inner-most thoughts. Tell me what you want so I can fulfill all of your needs." By looking into her eyes, he looked into her inner-most being, her soul.

But he didn't stop there! He presumed to adventure down to her lips, probably after giving her a kiss on the nose. He describes her lips as a scarlet ribbon, a medium dark shade of pink-red. He took notice of the color of her lipstick. Her lips and her mouth were important to him. Why? Because she began to speak words that would make Clark Kent become Super Man. Words that would make him feel like the king he was inside. She talked to him like Delilah talked to Samson and Ruth talked to Boaz.

Proverbs 14:1 says "Every wise woman buildeth her house: but the foolish plucketh it down with her hands." Ladies, one of the ways you can help your husband is by saying good things to him and about him, because you are his "good thing."

> Whoso findeth a wife findeth a good thing, and obtaineth favor of the Lord. Proverbs 18:22 KJV

As his good thing, tell him something good. Tell him that you love him. Tell him what a wonderful man he is to you. Tell him he's an awesome father. He's your provider, protector, and priest. Even if he's none of those things, say it until he becomes all of those things.

> Speak those things that be not as though they were. Romans 4:17

Every wife has to be a woman of faith, always believing God for the best for her family. Acts 2:17 reminds us that when the Holy Spirit comes on the woman, she prophesies:

> In the last days, God says, I will pour out my Spirit on all people. Your sons and daughters will prophesy, your young men

> will see visions, your old men will dream dreams.

When you find out what his dreams are and what God is showing him in visions, it would be to your advantage if you prophesied to him. Use your God given abilities to make him better.

> But the one who prophesies speaks to people for their strengthening, encouraging and comfort. - 1 Corinthians 14:3

STRENGTH

make or become stronger

God has given the woman the power to make her man stronger or make him weaker. The power to make him or break him. The power to make him successful or make him a failure. Your words will provide the strength he needs to become all that God has created him to be.

Through her words, my wife has given me the strength I need to be an awesome husband, father, friend, pastor, author, and the man God created me to be in this world. Make your husband strong enough to carry the load of the family. After all, he's the foundation of the family, meaning God built him first. But he needs his helper (the wife) to help keep him strong, to be the rocks in concrete so the family can be built on a solid foundation.

ENCOURAGEMENT

The action of giving someone
support, confidence, or hope.

Regardless of how big, tall, or strong a man may look, we all need encouragement along the way. Encouragement is the Vitamin A to our ego. A man who doesn't get the support he needs from his wife will struggle tremendously in being who God created him to be. David was a man after God's own heart, but there were times when he needed support. For example, when Nabal refused to feed David and his men, it led him to attempt to do something he probably would have regretted for the rest of his life: killing Nabal and all of his men. But Abigail stepped into the situation:

> When Abigail saw David, she quickly got off her donkey and bowed down before David with her face to the ground. She fell at his feet and said: "Pardon your servant, my lord, and let me speak to you; hear what your servant has to say. Please pay no attention, my lord, to that wicked man Nabal. He is just like his name—his name means Fool, and folly goes with him. And as for me, your servant, I did not see the men my lord sent. And now, my lord, as surely as the Lord your God lives and as you live, since the Lord has kept you from

bloodshed and from avenging yourself with your own hands, may your enemies and all who are intent on harming my lord be like Nabal. And let this gift, which your servant has brought to my lord, be given to the men who follow you. "Please forgive your servant's presumption. The Lord your God will certainly make a lasting dynasty for my lord, because you fight the Lord's battles, and no wrongdoing will be found in you as long as you live. Even though someone is pursuing you to take your life, the life of my lord will be bound securely in the bundle of the living by the Lord your God, but the lives of your enemies he will hurl away as from the pocket of a sling. When the Lord has fulfilled for my lord every good thing he promised concerning him and has appointed him ruler over Israel, my lord will not have on his conscience the staggering burden of needless bloodshed or of having avenged himself. And when the Lord your God has brought my lord success, remember your servant." David said to Abigail, "PRAISE BE TO THE LORD, the God of Israel, who has sent you today to meet me. May you be blessed for your good judgment and for keeping me from bloodshed this day

> and from avenging myself with my own hands. Otherwise, as surely as the Lord, the God of Israel, lives, who has kept me from harming you, if you had not come quickly to meet me, not one male belonging to Nabal would have been left alive by daybreak." Then David accepted from her hand what she had brought him and said, "Go home in peace. I HAVE HEARD YOUR WORDS and granted your request." 1 Samuel 25:23-35 NIV

This is one of the most amazing stories of hope in the Bible. Because this woman understood what David needed, she later became David's wife and queen on the throne of Israel. She gave him the support, hope, and confidence that he would need to be king one day. So when your husband is feeling low, help him to adjust his crown by ENCOURAGING your man.

COMFORT

The easing or alleviation of a person's feelings of grief or distress.

Israel, God's chosen people, often found themselves in need of comfort. God says to them, "Comfort, comfort my people, says your God. Speak tenderly to Jerusalem, and proclaim to her that her hard service has been completed, that her sin has been paid for, that she has received from the Lord's hand double for all her sins" (Isaiah 40:1-2 NIV).

Just like God spoke comfort to His people, the children of Israel, likewise, the man needs his wife to speak comfort to him.

Most men who come to my counseling sessions reveal to me their number one and number two love languages, which are sex and words of affirmation. Both relieve him of the stress and grief he goes through being a man. No matter what the world around him says, if he can get the comfort from within, then he can deal with the pressures without.

Wives, take your husband's head and place it in your bosom. Rock him like a newborn baby. Rub his head and make all his troubles go away. It is hard to fight the battles life brings outside of the house and on the inside, too. When a man comes in from dealing with the responsibilities of life, he needs a soft place to lay his head. He needs a place of relaxation, contentment, enjoyment, and satisfaction. Reward him for his hard work, and he will work even harder for you and his family. Make love to him and not war. Men love to go out to battle, but they do not like to come home to battle. Be to him who God created you to be, his HELPER, and he will be to you all that you need him to be--your PROVIDER, PROTECTOR, and PRIEST.

If that wasn't enough, Solomon perceived to acknowledge the strength of her neck. Don't mistake 1st Peter 3:7 to mean the wife is a frail, fragile, weak, or impotent woman. Her strength is not in her muscles. She's powerful, smart, brilliant, intelligent, strong, able, confident, capable, unbreakable. This is what the Virtuous Woman looks like in Proverbs 31:

> STRENGTH and DIGNITY are her clothing and her position is strong and secure; And she smiles at the future [knowing that she and her family are prepared]. She opens her mouth in [skillful and godly] wisdom, And the teaching of kindness is on her tongue [giving counsel and instruction]. She looks well to how things go in her household, And does not eat the bread of idleness. Her children rise up and call her blessed (happy, prosperous, to be admired); Her husband also, and he praises her, saying, "Many daughters have done nobly, and well [with the STRENGTH of character that is steadfast in goodness], But you excel them all." Charm and grace are deceptive, and [superficial] beauty is vain, But a woman who fears the LORD [reverently worshiping, obeying, serving, and trusting Him with awe-filled respect], she shall be praised. Proverbs 31:25-30 AMP

Her strength is found from her neck up, not from her neck down. She can be the greatest blessing that God has ever given you when you see her as your partner and not your subordinate.

> So God created man in His own image, in the image and likeness of God He created him; male and female He created them. And God blessed them [granting them certain authority] and said to them, "Be fruitful, multiply, and fill the earth, and subjugate it [putting it under your power]; and rule over (dominate) the fish of the sea, the birds of the air, and every living thing that moves upon the earth." Genesis 1:27-28 AMP

So God blessed the man and the woman to work together. Both of them were blessed and had authority in the earth. When this unit works in unison with the plans of God, nothing shall be impossible for them.

> "I assure you and most solemnly say to you, whatever you bind [forbid, declare to be improper and unlawful] on earth shall have [already] been bound in heaven, and whatever you loose [permit, declare lawful] on earth shall have [already] been loosed in heaven. "Again I say to you, that if two believers on earth agree [that is, are of one mind, in harmony] about anything that they ask [within the will of God], it will be done for them by My Father in heaven." Matthew 18:18-19 AMP

She has the ability to be strong IN BETWEEN THE SHEETS and in the streets. Solomon understood the strength of his wife. She helped him to be a man of integrity, because she was clothed with strength.

After Solomon had acknowledged how beautiful his wife's eyes, hair, teeth, lips, mouth, and neck were, then he got to the parts most men like. Notice brothers, he didn't start there, but he ended up there because God designed the woman's breasts to be a delight to her husband.

> "[Confine yourself to your own wife.] Let your children be yours alone, And not the children of strangers with you. Let your fountain (wife) be blessed [with the rewards of fidelity], And rejoice in the wife of your youth. Let her be as a loving hind and graceful doe, Let her breasts refresh and satisfy you at all times; Always be exhilarated and delight in her love. Why should you, my son, be exhilarated with an immoral woman And embrace the bosom of an outsider (pagan)?" Proverbs 5:17-20 AMP

God is saying, "I created her breasts to be for the husband's pleasure, that both of them might get pleasure out of them."

The Bible does not consider the breast a shameful part of the body. Breasts are rejoiced as a blessing. Breasts are celebrated for feeding children and even Jesus. Breasts are for a husband.

I'll end this part of Solomon's journey by reminding women to follow the leading of the Holy Spirit as they pursue this new freedom in the Word. Just because we realize we have been restricted by legalism and unnecessary rules does not allow us to disregard the leading of the Holy Spirit. Be free from the shame that keeps you from feeding your babies. Be free from the legalism. Yet cling to the Holy Spirit and pray for guidance on how you will proceed.

Solomon continued to make love to the mind of his wife. He said something to her that every woman wants to hear.

> "O my love, you are altogether beautiful and fair. There is no flaw nor blemish in you!" - Song of Solomon 4:7

As a person who has had several conditions that left me with scars on my body, I was pondering why society has programmed us to feel ashamed of our scars and tells us that we need to "fix" them. The conclusion I reached? We have been programmed to see any scar or flaw on our skin as ugly and abnormal—not beautiful as defined in the media. We have been taught to seek out solutions to remove or greatly diminish the appearance of these unacceptable scars through any means necessary—plastic surgery, laser therapy, scar gel, stretch mark creams—that we must "fix" our scars in order to fit in.

What if we could look at scars differently—see them from a different, more positive perspective? This would certainly be a challenge to the ideals that have been programmed into us through the media. What if we looked at scars/disfigurations as signs of strength and perseverance for those who have been through fires, accidents, or surgery—as a symbol of an individual's strength and ability to make it through a difficult and trying time? What about stretch marks from childbirth? Wouldn't it be great if we looked at stretch marks post-pregnancy as a "beauty" mark given to women by their child?

As a woman said "I think scars are like battle wounds — beautiful, in a way. They show what you've been through and how strong you are for coming out of it."

Yes, having scars/disfigurations means that we are not "perfect," but scars do not affect who we are on the inside, nor are we supposed to be perfect or flawless.

Scars and disfigurations do not define us. We should not feel ashamed to wear shorts or a bathing suit in the summer, or for those who have more disfiguring scars, to be in public.

For those who have scars, remember they are a part of who you are and should be accepted as such. They are beautiful in their own way. In terms of my own scars, I am not ashamed of my scars; I am ashamed of the world for not understanding.

My challenge to you is this: next time you see someone with scars, burns, or other disfigurements, instead of thinking of them as "abnormal" or ugly, try reflecting on the possible strength and beauty behind those scars. See their scars as beautiful, not something that must be "fixed." For that matter, try looking at your own scars this way as well.

Solomon saw his wife as all together lovely, flawless, immaculate, beautiful, spotless, unblemished, perfect. She was his good thing. "He who finds a [true and faithful] wife finds a good thing And obtains favor and approval from the LORD" (Proverbs 18:22 AMP). Maybe she had flaws, but we will never know because Solomon only saw the beauty in his bride.

The last thing I would like to discuss about Solomon and his bride is that they had a totally enjoyable and fulfilling sex life.

> "Now as to the matters of which you wrote: It is good (beneficial, advantageous) for a man not to touch a woman [outside marriage]. But because of [the temptation to participate in] sexual immorality, let each man have his own wife, and let each woman have her own husband. The husband must fulfill his [marital] duty to his wife [with good will and kindness], and likewise the wife to her husband. The wife does not have [exclusive] authority over her own body, but the husband shares

> with her; and likewise the husband does not have [exclusive] authority over his body, but the wife shares with him. Do not deprive each other [of marital rights], except perhaps by mutual consent for a time, so that you may devote yourselves [unhindered] to prayer, but come together again so that Satan will not tempt you [to sin] because of your lack of self-control."
> 1 Corinthians 7:1-5 AMP

I will never forget the time I was counseling a young couple concerning sex from God's point of view. I showed them this chapter about God's perspective on sex between the husband and wife. The wife couldn't believe God had so much to say about the subject of sex. I told her, after all God created the human body.

> "Then God said, "Let Us (Father, Son, Holy Spirit) make man in Our image, according to Our likeness [not physical, but a spiritual personality and moral likeness]; and let them have complete authority over the fish of the sea, the birds of the air, the cattle, and over the entire earth, and over everything that creeps and crawls on the earth." So God created man in His own image, in the image and likeness of God He created him; male and female He created them. And God blessed them

> [granting them certain authority] and said to them, "Be fruitful, multiply, and fill the earth, and subjugate it [putting it under your power]; and rule over (dominate) the fish of the sea, the birds of the air, and every living thing that moves upon the earth."" Genesis 1:26-28 AMP

She was amazed by what God had to say concerning sex in marriage. The only time God had a problem with sex is when the man and woman were not in the covenant of marriage.

> "Marriage is to be held in honor among all [that is, regarded as something of great value], and the marriage bed undefiled [by immorality or by any sexual sin]; for God will judge the sexually immoral and adulterous." Hebrews 13:4 AMP

The Father God who created us as sexual beings wants us to enjoy the beauty of sex.

Listen to Solomon describe his life of pleasuring his wife.

> "How beautiful is your love, my sister, my [promised] bride! How much better is your love than wine, And the fragrance of your oils Than all kinds of balsam and spices. Your lips, my [promised] bride, drip honey [as the honeycomb]; Honey

> and milk are under your tongue, And the fragrance of your garments is like the fragrance of Lebanon. A garden enclosed is my sister, my [promised] bride—A rock garden locked, a spring sealed up." Song of Solomon 4:10-12 AMP

I believe Solomon is saying, his wife is a closed-up fountain whose fluids are dying to be released. As the husband, his job is to remove the rocks so her waters can flow. Solomon wanted to unlock her garden and unseal her spring, so that she could enjoy the pleasures of a healthy marriage.

Most men have never been taught love and sex from God's perspective. Our sex education comes from what we heard in the streets from a lying friend or from T.V., magazines, or pornography--never really hearing it from the One Who created it. Like most of us when we buy something new, we never read the instruction manual; we just assume we know how to work it. In doing so, we never get the maximum out of what we have in our possession. Solomon is saying to the man, don't just unwrap her and not read the manufacturer's instruction manual that goes along with her.

Peter said "Likewise, ye husbands, dwell with them according to knowledge, giving honour unto the wife, as unto the weaker vessel, and as being heirs together of the grace of life; that your prayers be not hindered" (1 Peter 3:7 KJV). The more information you have as a husband, the better your marriage will be.

Peter is saying, don't just dwell with your wife, but dwell with her according to knowledge.

> "my people are destroyed from lack of knowledge. Because you have rejected knowledge, I also reject you as my priests; because you have ignored the law of your God, I also will ignore your children." Hosea 4:6 NIV

Marriages are dying every day because people don't know what they're doing and what is required to make it work.

> And Adam knew Eve his wife; and she conceived, and bare Cain, and said, I have gotten a man from the Lord. Genesis 4:1 KJV

Men, when we know our wives, then and only then can we come together and produce something awesome in our lives. When you know her, you will know every aspect, quality, component, feature about her nature. What makes her happy or sad? What are her dreams, goals, aspirations? What is her shoe size? What size is her dress? What size is her ring finger? What's her favorite food? What's her favorite color? The size of her bra?

All of these things every man needs to know, and it states it in between the sheets.

> "But he that is married careth for the things that are of the world, how he may please his wife." 1 Corinthians 7:33 KJV

How can you surprise your wife with the things she loves if you don't know her? Don't use the excuse that she is materialistic. She is materialistic because she lives in a material world and she is a material girl. That is one of the reasons why God gave Adam a job before He gave him a wife (see Genesis 2:15); Adam needed to have his coins in place so he could provide for her needs.

Likewise, wives, it is required of you to know your husband. All the things I mentioned that he needs to know, you need to know his needs as well.

> "There is difference also between a wife and a virgin. The unmarried woman careth for the things of the Lord, that she may be holy both in body and in spirit: but she that is married careth for the things of the world, how she may please her husband."
> 1 Corinthians 7:34 KJV

God's design is for both the husband and the wife to be fulfilled in the marriage.

> "Beloved, I wish above all things that thou mayest prosper and be in health, even as thy soul prospereth." 3 John 1:2

God's desire is for you to prosper in every area of your life, and that includes your sex life.

LADIES FIRST

Men, we have been taught all our lives to allow women to be first: to go through the door first; to get into the car first; to get on elevators before us. What if you took this same approach into the bedroom? I will please my wife before I please myself. I will find out what she needs to be totally happy in the bedroom, even if I have to ask her.

Unlike Solomon, God has given you one assignment, one wife to please.

Listen to the extent that Solomon pleases his wife: "A fountain of gardens," "a well of living waters," and "streams from Lebanon."

Solomon knew the secret of how to give his wife total fulfillment, to bring her to a utopia unlike anything she could experience in any other place in her life. He gave her total satisfaction because he knew her from the top of her head to the soles of her feet. He meticulously gave attention to her every detail of her body. Her hair, eyes, lips, teeth, neck, breast, vulva. Solomon left no stones unturned.

> Awake, O north wind; and come, thou south; blow upon my garden, that the spices thereof may flow out. Let my beloved come into his garden, and eat his

> pleasant fruits." Song of Solomon 4:15-16 KJV

Whatever it took to give his wife the satisfaction she needed to experience total fulfillment, he was willing to do. He blew on her garden so carefully and lightly that her spices began to flow. She experienced what most women never experience: being "omg," totally satisfied by her husband. Surely, she probably fell into a deep sleep after experiencing such an amazing orgasm.

> "When you lie down, you will not be afraid; When you lie down, your sleep will be sweet." Proverbs 3:24 AMP

I believe God puts this assignment into the hands of the husband. Make love to her so well that her sleep will be sweet because she is having dreams about you. Start enjoying the gift God has given to those who are married.

Please don't stop here. Continue reading to find out more of the secrets to having total fulfillment in your marriage. What you are looking for can truly be found in between the sheets.

CHAPTER FOUR

When Love is Not Enough

A couple came into my office one afternoon devastated about the events that had occurred in their marriage. The wife was so disappointed she had taken off her wedding ring. She said to me, "Pastor, I just can't do this anymore. It's not that I don't love my husband, but at this point, love is not enough." What she was saying was, "we need more to work with."

In the previous chapter, we talked about the importance of love in your relationship. So the question must be asked: why do people who love one another divorce?

The above couple's problem wasn't their lack of love, but their inability to know ***how*** to love one another. Hosea 4:6 says, "My people are destroyed for lack of knowledge." The word "knowledge" can be defined as "facts, information, and skills acquired by a person through experience or education; the theoretical or practical understanding of a subject."

If we can be honest with ourselves, very few of us have been taught how to truly love. We don't know what that word truly means.

I believe the hardest thing to do is something we have never seen. The easiest thing to do is something we ***have*** seen. In Ephesians 5:21-31, Paul lays out a plan to teach us what love really looks like. Love is not an emotional feeling that has the ability to change day by day. Love is a decision. You must choose to love.

There are approximately 109 million singles living in the United States. Fifty-three percent are women and Forty-seven percent are men. God gives us the ability to choose. God didn't choose Eve for Adam; He only created her. It was Adam who said in Genesis 2:23, "This is now bone of my bone and flesh of my flesh. She shall be called Woman because She was taken out of Man." God created a helper and Adam made her his wife.

In Ephesians 5:21, Paul tells the man and the woman to submit to one another in the fear of God. Marriage works so much better when the man and woman work together as a team. There is an old saying, "there's no I in team." We work together to help fulfill our purpose on Earth. Remember, it's teamwork that makes the dream work. We work together to accomplish each other's dreams.

In Genesis 1:26, God created Man and Woman in His image and likeness. He gave both the man and the woman dominion "over the birds of the air, the fish of the sea, and over everything that creepeth upon the face of the Earth," but there was one important exception: He never gave either one dominion over the other. They were both created to submit to God.

In Ephesians 5:22-33, the Apostle Paul lays out the responsibilities of love to both the woman and the man. In verse 22, God asked the wives to "submit to their own husbands as unto the Lord." What was He asking her to do? He was asking her to submit to his love. In the same way, God asks us to submit to His love. God is not a dictator over His people, and neither should the husband be over his wife.

Verse 25 tells the husband his responsibility to his wife: to love her like Christ loves the church. Christ doesn't make the church love Him. He uses something called "goodness" to make us fall in love with Him.

> not knowing it is goodness of God that leadeth us to repentance. - Romans 2:4b

When we see how good God is and what He has done for us, it makes us want to fall in love with Him. So it is with the wife; when she sees your agape love for her, submitting will not be an issue.

A woman is an incubator. Whatever you give her, she will take it in and give you back more than you gave her. If you give her a word, she will give you a sentence. If you give her a sentence, she will give you a paragraph. If you give her paragraph, she will give you a book. If you give her food, she will give you a meal. If you give her a house, she will give you a home. If you give her sperm, she will give you a baby. So men, if you put agape love in the incubator, you will get much more than what you put into her.

The problem arises when we put the wrong stuff into the incubator. We get back what we don't want to receive.

> It is better to dwell on the corner of a house top, than with a brawling woman in a wide house. - Proverbs 21:9

> It is better to dwell in the Desert than in a house with a continuous and angry woman. - Proverbs 21:19

This is why the Lord urges men to love their wives as Christ loved the church.

Sisters, don't ever look at your responsibility to submit to the man as being the greater responsibility. The Lord has required the man to do much more in the position of head of the family. He is required to love you like Christ loved the church. Also, he is asked to give himself for the family. Like Christ, he is to make the greatest sacrifice for the family. He is required to wash you with the water of the word of God. He is to love you like he loves his own body. He is required to love you like he loves himself. Then God asked the wife to respect her husband.

GRACE FOR THE RACE

I don't believe any marriage can make it "until death do us part" without grace. The reason I believe this is because one of my definitions of "marriage" is "a system by means of which persons who are sinful by nature and contentious are so caught up by a dream and purpose bigger than themselves that they work through the years, in spite of repeated disappointments and failures, to make the dream come true."

With this in mind, we need "grace for the race."

> But by the Grace of God I am what I am: and his grace which was bestowed upon me was not in vain: but I labored more abundantly than they all: yet not I, but the Grace of God which was with me. - Romans 15:10

Those who enter into a covenant relationship called marriage will need grace to make it to the end without a shadow of a doubt. There will be good days and bad days, ups and downs, changes and turnarounds. Every day won't be sunshine, but it's because of the rain that things grow. Grace helps us make it through the rainy days of our lives.

> but those who marry will face many troubles in this life. - 1 Corinthians 7:28b

God's grace is His kindness toward Mankind. God's Grace is sufficient for our lives (2 Corinthians 12:9).

Just like God extends His grace toward us, likewise we should extend kindness toward one another.

THE RESULT OF GRACE

Grace in the house will lead to peace. Paul said to the Romans, "Grace and peace to you from God our Father and from the Lord Jesus Christ" (Romans 1:7). If you want peace in the house, grace must be in the house. We must show the same kindness to one another as God has shown to us. Peace is not something that just happens; it's something we make happen. We made peace with God by accepting Him. We make peace in our marriages by showing grace in the house.

> Who is wise and understanding among you? Let them show it by their good life, by deeds done in the humility that comes from wisdom. But if you harbor bitterness and selfish ambition in your hearts , do not boast about it or deny the truth. Such "Wisdom" does not come down from Heaven but is earthly, unspiritual, demonic. For where you have envy and self-ambition, there you find disorder and every evil practice. But the Wisdom that comes from heaven is first of all pure; then

> peace-loving, considerate, submissive, full of mercy and good fruit, impartial and sincere. Peacemakers who sow in peace reap a harvest of righteousness. - James 3:13-18

Galatians 6:7 reminds us, "Do not be deceived: God cannot be mocked. A man reaps whatever he sows." If we want to see peace in our lives than we must sow peace in others. This is God's promise to us, "I will keep them in perfect peace whose mind is stayed on me" (Isaiah 26:3). So let us keep our minds on God's word and do what His Word says do. Then God's peace will flood our lives.

PEACE LEADS TO PROSPERITY

PROSPERITY and peace go together like a hand and glove. You cannot have one without the other. King David wrote in Psalms 122:6-7 "Pray for the peace of Jerusalem: they shall prosper that love thee. Peace be within thy walls, and prosperity within thy palaces."

When a house has peace within it, PROSPERITY will find its way to that house. PROSPERITY isn't just money--it's good health, wealth, success, comfort, security, plenty, and well-being. Your marriage will flourish, thrive, and have great success.

There are many marriages that have money and end up in divorce. Money alone will not keep a marriage, but if you have God's grace, grace will lead to peace, and peace will lead to PROSPERITY. Like Paul, you too can say "But by the Grace of God I am what I am."

DEFEATING DIVORCE
(Matthew 19:3-6)

In America, there is one divorce approximately every 36 seconds. That's nearly 2,400 divorces per day, 16,800 per week and 876,000 per year. The average length of a marriage that ends in divorce is eight years. People wait an average of three years after a divorce to remarry (if they remarry at all).

To say the least, our country has an epidemic called "divorce." 50 percent of all marriages end in divorce. What a staggering statistic to something that is truly important! Next to our decision of salvation, accepting Jesus Christ as Lord and Savior of our lives, marriage is the second most important decision you will make in your lifetime. This decision will affect every area of your life.

The spiritual challenges you will face as a divorcee can be innumerable. Those challenges can be so great, they can even make you question your faith in God. *How did God allow this to happen to me? If God is so good, why am I experiencing a life so bad? Why didn't God stop this from happening?* The questions in your mind can go on forever.

THE ANSWER FOR DIVORCE

I believe God has an answer for the divorce epidemic. Matthews 19:3-6 says,

> Some Pharisees came to Jesus to test him. They asked, "Is it lawful for a man to divorce his wife for any and every reason?" "Haven't you read," he replied, "that at the beginning the Creator 'made them male and female,' and said, 'For this reason a man will leave his father and mother and be united to his wife, and the two will become one flesh'?

Jesus said something very astonishing concerning divorce: *"Haven't you read?"* I believe one of the greatest reasons people get a divorce is the lack of knowledge. They enter into marriage with no idea what it will take to finish the journey.

Most people think love will save their marriage. That's not true. Love isn't enough to save a marriage. People who love each other divorce every day. It's not a lack of love, but a lack of information on how to love one another.

Most of us buy products but never read the full manufacturer's manual. We read the quick setup version. We do the same thing when it comes to marriage. We fall in love today, get married tomorrow, and get a divorce next week. The quick setup method doesn't work for marriage.

Wouldn't it be more beneficial to us if we sat down and familiarized ourselves with the manual before we began to operate the product? The manual would tell us the warranty, warnings, and guarantees of the product. The warning might say, "improper setup and care of this product can increase the risk of serious injury, device damage, or even death."

Marriage comes with the same warnings. If we do not set it up correctly (the original model) and take good care of it, it could lead to serious injuries of the mind, body, and spirit, or to the death of the marriage, also known as divorce.

In fact, divorce is worse than death. I've performed over 100 funerals. Funerals are heartbreaking and traumatizing. But after the funeral, people go through a grieving process. This is the grief model we call the 7 Stages of Grief:

Stage 1: Shock & Denial

You will probably react to learning of the loss with numbed disbelief. Grief is an overwhelming emotion. It's not unusual to respond to the intense and often sudden feelings by pretending the loss or change isn't happening. Denying it gives you time to gradually absorb the news and begin to process it. This is a common defense mechanism and helps numb you to the intensity of the situation.

As you move out of the denial stage, however, the emotions you've been hiding will begin to rise. You'll be confronted with a lot of the sorrow you've denied. That is also part of the journey of grief, but it can be difficult.

Stage 2: Anger

Where denial may be considered a coping mechanism, anger is a masking effect. Anger is hiding many of the emotions and pain you carry. This anger may be directed at other people, such as the person who died, your ex, or your old boss. You may even aim your anger at inanimate objects.

While your rational brain knows the object of your anger isn't to blame, your feelings in that moment are too intense to understand this.

Anger may not be clear-cut fury or rage. It may mask itself in feelings like bitterness or resentment. Not everyone will experience this stage. Some may linger here. As the anger subsides, however, you may begin to think more rationally about what's happening and feel the emotions you've been pushing aside.

Stage 3: Bargaining

During grief, you may feel vulnerable and helpless. In those moments of intense emotions, it's not uncommon to look for ways to regain control or to feel like you can affect the outcome of an event. In the bargaining stage of grief, you may find yourself creating a lot of "what if" and "if only" statements.

It's also not uncommon for religious individuals to try to make a deal or promise to God or a higher power in return for healing or relief from the grief and pain. Bargaining is a line of defense against the emotions of grief. It helps you postpone the sadness, confusion, or hurt.

Stage 4: Depression

Whereas anger and bargaining can feel very "active," depression may feel like a "quiet" stage of grief.

In the early stages of loss, you may be running from the emotions, trying to stay a step ahead of them. By this point, however, you may be able to embrace and work through them in a more healthful manner. You may also choose to isolate yourself from others in order to fully cope with the loss.

That doesn't mean, however, that depression is easy or well defined. Like the other stages of grief, depression can be difficult and messy. It can feel overwhelming. You may feel foggy, heavy, and confused.

Depression may feel like the inevitable landing point of any loss. However, if you feel stuck here or can't seem to move past this stage of grief, talk with a mental health expert. A therapist can help you work through this period of coping.

Stage 5: The Upward Turn

At this point, the stages of grief like anger and pain have died down, and you're left in a more calm and relaxed state.

Stage 6: Reconstruction & Working Through

You can begin to put pieces of your life back together and carry forward.

Stage 7: Acceptance & Hope

Acceptance is not necessarily a happy or uplifting stage of grief. It doesn't mean you've moved past the grief or loss. It does, however, mean that you've accepted it and have come to understand what it means in your life now.

You may feel very different in this stage. That's entirely expected. You've had a major change in your life, and that upends the way you feel about many things. Look to acceptance as a way to see that there may be more good days than bad, but there may still be bad — and that's OK.

After going through these stages, one can begin to put one's life back together again. But it's not so easy when it comes to divorce. Divorce is the living dead.

Jesus said, "the two shall become one flesh (Matthew 19:5)." My illustration of divorce is taking a chainsaw and splitting a person from the top of their head down the middle of their body, which would lead to a bloody mess. Divorce is bloody and messy.

Nobody wins when it comes to divorce. So many people are affected by the decision. Family, friends, co-workers, church members, not to mention children, who are affected the most.

A marriage needs more than love. It needs knowledge, wisdom, information, and understanding.

> "Hear, O children, the instruction of a father, And pay attention [and be willing to learn] so that you may gain understanding and intelligent discernment. For I give you good doctrine; Do not turn away from my instruction. When I was a son with my father (David), Tender and the only son in the sight of my mother (Bathsheba), He taught me and said to me, "Let your heart hold fast my words; Keep my commandments and live. Get [skillful and godly] wisdom! Acquire understanding [actively seek spiritual discernment, mature comprehension, and logical interpretation]! Do not forget nor turn away from the words of my mouth. Do not turn away from her (Wisdom) and she will guard and protect you; Love her, and she will watch over you. The beginning of wisdom

> is: Get [skillful and godly] wisdom [it is preeminent]! And with all your acquiring, get understanding [actively seek spiritual discernment, mature comprehension, and logical interpretation]. Prize wisdom [and exalt her], and she will exalt you; She will honor you if you embrace her. She will place on your head a garland of grace; She will present you with a crown of beauty and glory."" - Proverbs 4:1-9 AMP

King Solomon, the greatest lover of all time, lets us know in addition to love, a marriage needs wisdom to fulfill its purpose. Wisdom is the soundness of an action or decision with regard to the application of experience, knowledge, and good judgment. It is also the body of knowledge and principles that develop within a specified society or period. Every man and woman needs wisdom if their marriage is going to reach its full potential. Proverbs 14:1 says, "The wise woman builds her house, but with her own hands the foolish one tears hers down."

> "A man without wisdom enjoys being foolish. But a man with understanding does what is right. Plans fail without good advice. But plans succeed when you get advice from many others. People enjoy giving good answers! Saying the right word at the right time is so pleasing! A

> wise person does things that will make his life better. He avoids whatever would cause his death (Divorce)." - Proverbs 15:21-24 ICB

So the question is, how do we get wisdom?

James 1:5 says, "If any of you lacks wisdom [to guide him through a decision or circumstance], he is to ask of [our benevolent] God, who gives to everyone generously and without rebuke or blame, and it will be given to him."

God will give you the wisdom you need to help you in the difficult times of your marriage when love is not enough.

Solomon also said, "get knowledge." Knowledge is facts, information, and skills acquired by a person through experience or education; the theoretical or practical understanding of a subject. It is important that you get the information you need to make your marriage work. Again, one of my favorite scriptures in the Bible is Hosea 4:6, "my people are destroyed from lack of knowledge. Because you have rejected knowledge, I also reject you as my priests; because you have ignored the law of your God, I also will ignore your children" (NIV).

I believe your marriage will either live or die based on the knowledge you have about marriage.

> Some Pharisees came to him to test him. They asked, "Is it lawful for a man to

> divorce his wife for any and every reason?" "Haven't you read," he replied, "that at the beginning the Creator 'made them male and female,'" - Matthew 19:3-4 NIV

Jesus, the originator of marriage, said the answer to the divorce question is knowledge. "Haven't you read?" When we read, we gather information, facts, and education on how to be married. There are more books than you will ever be able to read on the subject of marriage. Don't ever stop educating yourself. There is always something new to be learned about the subject. I'm sure if you've read this far in this book, you've probably learned something new to apply to your marriage.

Solomon also said, "in all of your getting, get understanding." Understanding can be defined by the ability to understand something; comprehension. Also, sympathetically aware of other people's feelings; tolerant and forgiving, having insight or good judgment. Having understanding in a marriage will go a long way when love runs a little low. Understanding can keep your marriage alive when you don't fully get what's going on with your spouse. You can still be sympathetic to their feelings. Add wisdom, knowledge, and understanding to your love for your spouse so you can make it to the finish line.

CHAPTER FIVE

Restoring the Broken Pieces

When I was 12 years old, our house burned down. A storm had knocked out the power, and an unsecured candle caught fire. I remember waking up to a house filled with smoke. In panic mode, I jumped from the top of the stairs to the bottom, hoping to get out alive. Our family barely made it out of that fire. All we had were the clothes on our backs. But thank God we made it out of that house alive.

A few days later, after the fire went out, I remember my grandfather, Emmitt Melvin, raking through ashes looking for money he often kept in the house. He was trying to find what he thought was valuable, worth saving.

Many couples come into my office after spending 20 or 30 years together asking the same questions as my grandfather. *Is there anything worth saving? Is there anything left? Can we find a reason to continue this marriage?* The children are grown and the love has dissipated over the years. It seems as though all we had has turned into rubble.

Many marriages over the years have encountered hurts, heartache, pain, distrust, infidelity, and/or abuse. Often, spouses look over their lives and ask the questions, "Can this marriage be restored?" "Can we love again?" "Can we sift through the rubble of this marriage and find something worth saving?"

Let's take a look at Nehemiah and how he dealt with the devastation of the walls of Jerusalem being broken down and the gates being burned with fire.

In hearing this news, Nehemiah wept. I believe God has given us the ability to cry to release built up emotion, pain, and hurts we experience in our lives.

Psalms 30:5b says "weeping may endure for a night, but joy cometh in the morning." Before we can begin to rebuild our lives, we must give ourselves permission to acknowledge the pain.

Too often, we've been told crying is a sign of weakness. I beg the differ. If crying were a sign of weakness, then ask yourself, "is Jesus weak?" There were times the Son of God wept. When He looked over Jerusalem and saw it as if it were sheep having no shepherd and the people were devastated, He wept. He also cried over the loss of His friend, Lazarus. At Lazarus' grave, when He felt the pain of Lazarus' sisters, Mary and Martha, and wept (John 11:35).

But not only did the strong man Jesus cry, but the mighty warrior king David cried as well. When David and his men saw the city of Ziglag burned to the ground and their wives and children were kidnapped, David and the 400 mighty men of valor cried until they had no power to weep (I Samuel 30:3-4). This is the same David who killed the giant by the name of

Goliath. It was also said in Jerusalem, "King Saul killed his thousands but David killed his ten thousands" (1 Samuel 18:7 KJV). This man was no one to play with, but he gave himself permission to cry after experiencing a great loss.

So, especially to the men, I know they told us that we're not supposed to cry, but I don't believe they told us the truth. This is why we do things out of anger many times. Instead of crying, we take out our frustrations on others. Maybe if we could find another avenue to channel those emotions into, we could avoid adding to the devastation we are already dealing with.

Nehemiah found other weapons to deal with the broken-down walls and burned up gates: fasting and prayer. Fasting is a powerful tool that we don't use a lot anymore. I never make a major decision in my life without a time of fasting. Fasting helps bring you into focus. It also draws you closer to God.

Isaiah 58:6 says the kind of fasting that God has chosen will "loose the chains of injustice, untie the cords of the yoke, to set the oppressed free, and break every yoke" (NIV).

Fasting prepares you to be able to build your life again. Jesus, before He launched His ministry, spent 40 days in the wilderness fasting. I believe it was to prepare Himself for the 3-and-a-half year journey He was about to go on.

If you're going to rebuild your marriage, expect to go on a journey to do it. It didn't get to this place overnight and it won't be rebuilt overnight.

One couple who came to my office committed themselves to over three years of consistently coming to marriage counseling and I dare to say it has turned their lives and marriage all the way around, to the extent they have added another child to their family. To God be the glory for the great things He has done. Try fasting and reap the results of it.

Nehemiah also prayed to God. Prayer is one of the most powerful tools God has given to man. Prayer is an invitation to have intimacy with God, an opportunity to talk to God and tell Him all that is going on in your heart. He understands you better than anyone on earth. Why? Because He Himself had to deal with rejection. "He came unto his own and his own received him not" (John 1:11).

He also dealt with being misunderstood. They called him Beelzebub, the chief of demons (Matthew 12:24; Mark 3:22). He went through being beaten and wounded for our sins. Thirty-nine lashes with the cat o' nine tails He took for our healing. Hebrews 4:15 says "we do not have a high priest who is unable to empathize with our weaknesses, but we have one who has been tempted in every way, just as we are--yet, he did not sin" (NIV).

When we go to God, we must know He can understand just how we feel. He gives us an open invitation morning, noon, and night. My mother Shirley Matthews' favorite scripture was Matthew 11:28-30:

> "Come unto me all you who are weary and heavy burdened, and I will give you rest. Take my yoke upon you and learn from me, for I am gentle in heart, and you will find rest for your souls. For my yoke is easy and my burdens are light."

Prayer helps lift the heavy burdens, gives us rest and a place of peace for our souls. When our souls are at peace, we can make better decisions and achieve greater victories. Jesus taught in a parable in Luke 18:1 men ought to always pray and not quit.

Prayer gives us the power, the ability, to persevere through the greatest challenges and troubles of our lives. Without prayer, maintaining a marriage or rebuilding one will be a difficult task to say the least.

The one thing I love the most about my wife, Sheila Melvin, after 30 years of marriage is her love for God and the prayer life she has with Him. There are things she gets from God I would never be able to achieve. If a man is wise, he will never try to be his wife's all in all. The greatest gift he can give her is not money, gold, diamonds, or pearls. It's not even himself.

Brothers, let us check our egos. The most important gift you can give your spouse is to encourage them to have a relationship with Jesus Christ. Their prayer and intimate time with the Master will be beneficial to both of you.

Nehemiah fasted and prayed before he attempted to rebuild the broken-down walls and burned up gates. Before you start to build or rebuild your marriage, prayer and fasting should be the foundation upon which you build.

Let's look at another principle you should build your marriage upon. After prayer and fasting was done, Nehemiah needed a plan of action. Fasting, prayer, or faith without action is dead. There must be a plan if you are going to have a successful marriage. There's an old saying "those who fail to plan, plan to fail." Even God does nothing without a plan.

> "I make known the end from the beginning, from ancient times, what is still to come. I say 'My purpose will stand, and I will do all that I please.'" - Isaiah 46:10

Because we are made in the image and likeness of God, He has given us the same ability to make plans and complete them. Nehemiah went to the king with a clear and precise plan of action. The book of Proverbs has a lot to say about the importance of planning:

> Many are the plans in a person's heart, but it is the Lord's purpose that prevails.
> - Proverbs 19:21 NIV

> A plan (motive, wise counsel) in the heart of a man is like water in a deep well, But a man of understanding draws it out. - Proverbs 20:5 AMP

> Plans are established by seeking advice; so if you wage war, obtain guidance. - Proverbs 20:18 NIV

> The plans of the diligent lead surely to abundance and advantage, But everyone who acts in haste comes surely to poverty. - Proverbs 21:5 AMP

> Proverbs 29:18 Where there is no revelation, (Plan) the people perish; but blessed is the one who heeds wisdom's instruction.

In Luke 14:28, Jesus, the master builder, tells us how to make our plans successful:

> "For which of you, intending to build a tower, sitteth not down first, and counteth the cost, whether he have sufficient to finish it?"

There are three significant steps in any successful building or rebuilding project and they are:

STEP #1: SIT DOWN

> Be still, and know that I am God: I will be exalted among the heathen, I will be exalted in the earth. - Psalms 46:10

Being still doesn't mean we are being idle; it means we don't rush into a situation. We take our time and get advice. We gather as much information as we possibly can. Why, you might ask? Because knowledge is power.

The scriptures reminds us, "My people are destroyed for lack of knowledge: because thou hast rejected knowledge, I will also reject thee, that thou shalt be no priest to me: seeing thou hast forgotten the law of thy God, I will also forget thy children" (Hosea 4:6).

Most relationships don't fail because of the lack of love; they fail simply because the people don't know what they're doing. After I've counseled many men and their relationships get better, they often come back to me and say, "it wasn't the fact I didn't love my wife but I just didn't know how to love her as God intended for me to love her." They made a decision to sit down first and get some wise counseling.

STEP # 2: COUNT THE COST

Nehemiah understood there would be an astronomical cost to rebuild the walls and gates of Jerusalem, but he didn't let that stop him. He knew the hand of the Lord was with him. If God be for us, who can be against us (Romans 8:31b)? Nehemiah understood that God's will always supersedes our plans.

Ephesians 3:20 says "Now unto him that is able to do exceeding abundantly above all that we ask or think, according to the power that worketh in us." Remember Proverbs 16:9: "In their hearts humans plan their course, but the Lord establishes their steps" (NIV). God is saying, "after you've made your plans, then I will get involved and do exceedingly abundantly above all that you can ask or think according to the power that works in you."

Anything worth having is worth you putting in your time, resources, money, mind, energy, gifts, and your life. That's probably why God gave Adam a job before He gave him a wife (see Genesis 2:15). When we realize everything has a cost to it, we should be willing to do all we can to make it succeed, because whether it succeeds or fails, there will still be a cost to our relationship. Divorce lawyers are getting rich off of people who didn't count the cost of marriage.

STEP #3: FINISH WHAT YOU STARTED

There's another quote that says, "It's not where you start; it's where you finish." I see so many relationships start out great, but after a few years, they begin to dissipate. Relationships have to be built on a solid foundation. What's the solid foundation our relationship should be built upon?

> "Therefore everyone who hears these words of mine and puts them into practice is like a wise man who built his house on the rock. The rain came down, the streams rose, and the winds blew and beat against that house; yet it did not fall, because it had its foundation on the rock. But everyone who hears these words of mine and does not put them into practice is like a foolish man who built his house on sand. The rain came down, the streams rose, and the winds blew and beat against that house, and it fell with a great crash." Matthew 7:24-27

Our relationships must be built on the word of God. God laid out His plan for relationships in His Word. We have a choice to make concerning our relationships. We can build them on a solid foundation, or we can build them on sand. Sand is what we want to do and how we want to do it. The solid foundation is God's word.

When the Pharisee asked Jesus about divorce in Matthews 19:3-9, the answer Jesus gave them was totally mind blowing. He gave them the key to all successful marriages.

Often, I ask couples to tell me what they believe are the keys to a successful marriage. Normally they give me the basic list everyone gives: love, trust, money, honesty, sex. Even though all of these are important, to my amazement, Jesus never mentioned one of these.

Love alone won't keep a marriage together. Jesus's response to the question was, "haven't you read?" He answered their question with a question. Jesus was telling them an essence. Your marriage will succeed or fail based on the knowledge you possess.

After counseling couples and helping them turn their marriages around, when our sessions are completed, I always ask them *What is the number one thing that has made a difference in your marriage?* The same answer consistently comes back: *The information we have received.* They often say, *"we simply did not know what we were doing."*

People do better based on the information they've received. If you want to keep people in the dark, take away their ability to ascertain knowledge. That's why God laid out His plan of action for the husband and wife, to let them know what their primary roles and responsibilities would be.

For example, the husband is to love his wife like Christ loved the church and gave himself for her. If a husband wants to know how to love his wife, he should take a good look at how Jesus Christ loved his bride, the church. So, I ask the husband, "*why do you think the majority of churches are filled with women?"* Most of the time their answer is, *"I don't know."* Then I further explain to them, the Lord gives them what they need."

My brother, these are the things she wants to hear and see you do. The husband is to love his bride like Christ loves his bride, the church. He should "wash her with the water of the word" and "present her to himself" as a radiant church (Bride), "without stain or wrinkle or any other blemish, but holy and blameless" (Ephesians 5:26-27 NIV).

Also the husbands "in this same way ought to love their wives as their own bodies. He who loves his wife loves himself" (Ephesians 5:28 NIV).

Over and over again, Ephesians chapter 5 tells the husband what the wife needs from him. These are the things the One who built her said she needs:

She needs to be loved.

She needs to be nourished. The word "nourish" means "to keep (a feeling or belief) in one's mind, typically for a long time." As long as she lives, she needs to hear and feel the love from her husband.

She also needs to be cherished. "Cherish" means "to treasure—to hold or treat something as dear and often loved." The word implies a deep and active appreciation of the person or thing that's cherished.

One of the responsibilities of the husband is to always make his wife feel treasured. She is valuable, precious, and of a great wealth. She is to be adored, admired, and appreciated. When she receives this, she will feel loved by her husband.

But wives, in order to get all of what you need, the husband must also feel loved, but in a different way.

He needs sex and respect.

Don't criticize him for wanting this from you. It's how he has been designed by God. God designed it in him to make sure he keeps populating the earth.

Right after sex, his next greatest need is RESPECT.

Every man has the need to be respected. If any person on the planet disrespects him, there will be consequences and repercussions. So God tells the wife she must respect her husband.

You might ask, how do I respect him? You give him special attention and honor. You compliment him and give him praise for the things he does. Don't just point out what he isn't doing; find things he is doing. Then you will have the right to show him what he needs to do. If you just criticize him all the time, it will kill him inside and he will not give you the love and affection you need.

Both the husband and the wife have needs that must be fulfilled. Once these are fulfilled, the broken pieces can be put back together again.

CHAPTER SIX

It's Not You, It's Me

Not long ago, a woman called my office and said "Pastor, I want to work on my marriage." I said "Well, when will you and your husband be coming into my office?" To my surprise, she replied, "Not with my husband; just me."

Up to this point, I wouldn't counsel couples individually. I thought I needed the other one there to find out where the problem truly was. However, the truth of the matter is some people just know they "need a little work."

For a year and a half, I helped this wife become single--separate yet attached to an individual. I helped her realize how uniquely God had created her, that she was fearfully and wonderfully made by God (Psalm 139:14). Before the foundation of the Earth, God finished everything about her. Like He told Jeremiah in Jeremiah 1:5, "before I formed you in the belly I knew you; and before you came forth out of your mother's womb I sanctified you, and I ordained you a prophet to the nations."

Often couples go to counseling hoping to fix the other person. But I begin to persuade them to take the "It's Not You, It's Me" approach.

I am a Seinfeld junkie. There's one episode where a couple didn't know how to break up with one another. They were looking for a way out. They would use the slogan "It's not you. It's me," meaning, there is something wrong with me, not you. What if couples took this slogan seriously? What would happen to their relationships? What would happen to their lives individually? What might they pass on to their children?

The couples I work with quickly begin to see this principle work. Matthew 7:3-5 states,

> Why do you look at the speck of sawdust in your brother's eye and pay no attention to the plank in your own eye? You hypocrite, first take the plank out of your own eye, and then you will see clearly to remove the speck from your brother's eye.

Removing the issues out of your life will make the relationship far greater than you could ever imagine.

We must understand that before we hooked up with our spouses, our purpose, destiny, and who we are had been pre-determined by God. The reason for the hook up is to help one another fulfill God's purposes and plans for our lives.

Being whole is one of the most important parts of our singleness. When God created us, He made us whole. 1 Thessalonians 5:23 says,

> And the God of peace sanctify your whole spirit and soul and body be preserved blameless unto the coming of our Lord Jesus Christ.

In order to be whole, you must work on each part of yourself: your spirit (that's the real you), your soul (your mind, will, and emotion), and your body (the temple that houses the spirit and the soul).

The trials and tribulations of life have done a job on our spirit, soul, and body. What we've inherited from previous generations has allowed us to be damaged goods. Being whole is allowing God to fix our broken spirit, bring peace to our minds, and bring healing to our bodies.

For example, if you have had a traumatic experience in your life such as abuse, abandonment, or being told you would never be anybody, especially from parents, mentors, or pastors, you need God's help to repair the brokenness that may have occurred in those situations. Professional counseling may be needed as well. Putting the broken pieces of your life back together will bless your relationship as a whole. Therefore, working on you will make the relationship so much better because you will be so much better.

Lastly, nobody knows what you have experienced in your life better than you do. You have to take control of your life and be the best you, period.

CHAPTER SEVEN

Don't Be Afraid to Show Your Wounds

> Man born of a woman is of few days and full of trouble. -Job 14:1

I'll never forget when I married my wife, God's gift to me, I thought I had married an angel. Until one day the wings fell off her back and the little horns came out of her head. She showed me a side of her I had never seen. I realized then that I had married a beautiful woman on the outside who was a damaged woman on the inside. The damage or baggage she was carrying affected our marriage.

Not to mention she also married a damaged man. A man who had been abandoned as a little boy by his father and mother, and was raised by his grandparents. As a result, I lived a life of anger, resentment, and low self-esteem, of always feeling less than, until one day I accepted Jesus Christ as the Lord and Savior of my life. I allowed Him to heal my past and brighten my future. Thank you Lord!

I had to realize the source of my pain so that I could get some medication for my problem. Until that occurred, I was self-medicating by drinking alcohol, smoking marijuana, and doing other things that would keep me from the reality of life.

When we understand that we all go through hurts, heartache, and pains, we don't take them personally. Troubles are just a part of life. They will either make us better or bitter, stronger or weaker, successful or a failure. Jesus said, "...In me you might have peace. In the world you shall have tribulation. But be of good cheer; I have overcome the world" (John 16:33). Because He has overcome the world, and all the problems it brings, we, too, can have victory in this life.

But being wounded and covering it up is not the answer. The wounds will eventually show themselves somewhere in our lives--on our jobs, in our churches, in our relationships, and especially in our homes. Wherever you go, when you get there, the wounded you will show up, too.

You might ask, "How, when I do such an amazing job covering up my wounds?" Here are a few examples of the wounded you showing up: outbursts of anger; low self-esteem; underachieving: and blaming others for the work we need to do on ourselves.

Jesus Christ was not afraid to show His wounds. In John 20:19-29, after He had been crucified and had risen on the third day, He appeared to His disciples and said "Peace be unto you" (v. 19). John 20:20 says Jesus showed them his hands and his side, the places where He was wounded.

I believe this is the area that stops us from having true intimacy, or how I like to spell it INTO-ME-SEE. When we allow those who are in relationships with us to see who we really are, then our relationships can take on greater meaning.

Isaiah 53:4-5 says, "Surely he took up our pain and bore our suffering, yet we considered him punished by God, stricken by him, and afflicted. But he was pierced for our transgressions, he was crushed for our iniquities; the punishment that brought us peace was on him, and by his wounds we are healed."

The question is, will we allow God to heal the wounds of our past, present, and future, or will we go through life covering up our wounds?

When Thomas saw Jesus's wounds, Jesus said to Thomas, "Put your finger here; see my hands. Reach out your hand and put it into my side. Stop doubting and believe" (John 20:27). Then Thomas cried out, "My Lord and my God" (v. 28)!

Showing your wounds allows others to know you are human.

CHAPTER EIGHT

We are Better Together

Over the last 30 years, my wife and I have faced many, many challenges in our marriage, challenges that include starting a home improvement business and founding a church. There were many tests we had to go through to fulfill God's will for our lives and the lives of others. But we always stayed on one accord, supporting one another's dreams, goals, and aspirations.

Ecclesiastes 4:9 says, "Two are better than one." God had a divine purpose in mind when He created them male and female (see Genesis 1:27). That purpose was to bless them. Together, they would be an unstoppable force in the earth. As long as they stayed in the Father's will, whatever they came into agreement with, they could accomplish.

> "Again I say unto you, that if two of you shall agree on earth as touching any thing that they shall ask, it shall be done for them of my Father which is in heaven. For where two or three are gathered together in my name, there am I in the midst of them." - Matthew 18:19-20 KJV

God is letting you know that as long as the two of you are in agreement, He will bless whatever you do. In fact, He said in 1 Peter 3:7-9,

> "Likewise, ye husbands, dwell with them according to knowledge, giving honour unto the wife, as unto the weaker vessel, and as being heirs together of the grace of life; that your prayers be not hindered. Finally, be ye all of one mind, having compassion one of another, love as brethren, be pitiful, be courteous: Not rendering evil for evil, or railing for railing: but contrariwise blessing; knowing that ye are thereunto called, that ye should inherit a blessing."

How amazing it is to know the LORD God will bless your togetherness?

This is the reason the enemy fights so hard to keep couples divided. He knows if you are on one accord, the two of you are going to be blessed. Strive to be together, on the same page, working with each other to fulfill your purpose on Earth, so that God's blessing can overflow in your life.

Keep the following principles in mind to stay on one accord with your spouse.

PRINCIPLE #1: SUPPORT ONE ANOTHER

One of the key principles of living in harmony with someone is believing the person you hook up with has your best interest at heart, and you have theirs. God wanted Adam and Eve to live in harmony with each other. That's why He didn't put one over the other. They were to work together as a unified team to accomplish God's purposes for themselves upon the earth. Too often, we focus more on ourselves than the person we're in a relationship with.

> Who is wise and understanding among you? Let them show it by their good life, by deeds done in the humility that comes from wisdom. But if you harbor bitter envy and selfish ambition in your hearts, do not boast about it or deny the truth. Such "wisdom" does not come down from heaven but is earthly, unspiritual, demonic. For where you have envy and selfish ambition, there you find disorder and every evil practice. But the wisdom that comes from heaven is first of all pure; then peace-loving, considerate, submissive, full of mercy and good fruit, impartial and sincere. Peacemakers who sow in peace reap a harvest of righteousness. - James 3:13-18

If we're going to have meaningful and productive relationships, we have to get rid of bitterness, envy, jealousy, and selfish ambitions. We must replace those things with being merciful, kind, impartial, sincere, and a peacemaker.

Are you a peacemaker in the relationship you're in, or do you cause strife and disorder? If you want peace in your relationship, you must sow peace to reap a life of good fruit.

> Do not be deceived: God cannot be mocked. A man reaps what he sows. Whoever sows to please their flesh, from the flesh will reap destruction; whoever sows to please the Spirit, from the Spirit will reap eternal life. Let us not become weary in doing good, for at the proper time we will reap a harvest if we do not give up. - Galatians 6:7-9

The Word is very clear: we get out of life what we put into it. This includes our relationships. If we sow negative things into our relationships, we will surely reap negative things out of them. On the other hand, if we sow positive things into our relationships, we will reap the benefits of those positive things which we have sown.

PRINCIPLE #2: VALUE YOUR SPOUSE ABOVE YOURSELF

Principle #2 is much like #1. If you're going to do all that needs to be done to make a relationship work, then you have to put a value on your relationship.

The definition of the word value is "the regard that something is held to deserve; the importance, worth, or usefulness of something." What we do not value we will not deem as important, significant, useful, beneficial, or worthy. You invest in things you value, things you believe will yield a return for your time, money, or resources.

Philippians 2:3-4 says, "Do nothing out of selfish ambition or vain conceit. Rather, in humility value others above yourselves."

God placed the value on our lives when He made the decision to die for our Sins.

> You see, at just the right time, when we were still powerless, Christ died for the ungodly. Very rarely will anyone die for a righteous person, though for a good person someone might possibly dare to die. But God demonstrates his own love for us in this: While we were still sinners, Christ died for us. - Romans 5:6-8

God valued His children so much that He was willing to die for them. What did He do? He put our needs far above Himself. In the garden of Gethsemane,

Jesus prayed this prayer:

> Father, if you are willing, take this cup from me; yet not my will, but yours be done. - Luke 22:42

Even though the cross was one of the most despicable ways to die, He did it because He believed we were worth it. When we honestly understand our spouse is a gift from God, then we will treat them like they need to be treated, giving them the love, support, and respect they truly deserve.

PRINCIPLES #3: HOW YOU DOING?

Talk show host Wendy Williams coined the phrase "How you doing?" No one has to teach us how to be selfish. We are naughty by nature. We have been taught to be self-centered and selfish from the cradle. My milk bottle, my bed, my room, my TV, my toys. Everything is about me, myself, and I.

Great relationships are not born out of the "what about me?" syndrome. The late great President John F. Kennedy once said, and I quote, "Ask not what your country can do for you-- ask what you can do for your country." We have to have the same mentality as our former president.

Honey, what can I do for you? What is it that you need from me? What can I help you with today? Is there anything I can do for you? In a good relationship, these questions must be asked. Because we have been put in a place of servanthood. We have been brought together to serve one another, to care for one another, to have one another's best interests at heart.

> Jesus called them together and said, "You know that those who are regarded as rulers of the Gentiles Lord it over them, and their high officials exercise authority over them. Not so with you. Instead, whoever wants to become great among you must be your servant, and whoever wants to be first must be slave of all. For even the Son of Man did not come to be served, but to serve, and to give his life as a ransom for many." - Mark 10:42-45

A true, loving relationship always asks *"what is it that I can give?"* not *"what will I receive?"* Jesus gave His life for His bride and reaped millions of souls as a result. What are you willing to give to your spouse?

Remember, we get out what we put in. If we want a great marriage, let's start by serving one another. Then we will reap a harvest of blessing. Have you asked your spouse how they are doing today? Go ahead. Give it a try. Don't be afraid. You will be amazed at the change in your marriage.

PRINCIPLE #4: FULFILL ONE ANOTHER'S PURPOSE

Even though we are part of a couple, we must not forget the fact we have our own individual goals, dreams, aspirations, and purposes. However, while we're focusing on our own interests, we must also remember our spouse has interests as well. Philippians 2:4-5 says, "not looking to your own interests but each of you to the interests of the others. In your relationships with one another, have the same mindset as Christ Jesus."

While Jesus was on the Earth, His focus was never centered on Himself, but what He could do to help and heal the suffering of mankind.

Jesus said in John 5:30, "By myself I can do nothing; I judge only as I hear, and my judgment is just, for I seek not to please myself but him who sent me." When you seek to please the one you're with, both of you will be pleased. So take the time to find out what your spouse's interests are.

If we keep these principles in our mind and marriage, then we can truly be better together.

CHAPTER NINE

Surviving the Marital Vows

Marital life is a marathon, not a sprint. If we are to finish strong, then we must survive the marital vows. The marital vows are the agreement we sign up for when we get married. Here's a reminder of them:

Officiant: "Will you have this (woman/man) to be your (wife/husband), to live together in holy marriage? Will you love (her/him), comfort (her/him), honor, and keep (her/him) in sickness and in health, for richer or poorer, for better or for worse and forsaking all others, be faithful to (her/him) as long as you both shall live?

For most of us, this is when the relationship gets real. *I'm making a lifelong commitment to another person. Wow!!!* The question has to come up in your mind, *Can I keep the vows I've just committed?*

I will never forget attending the wedding ceremony of one of my clients. He was all smiles before the ceremony began--until he got to the lifelong commitment. In the middle of the ceremony, the young man broke down and cried feverishly. The ceremony was held up until he could get himself together. After the wedding was over, I asked him what happened. *"It wasn't that I didn't love my wife,* he said, *but for the first time, the reality of honoring those vows hit* me *straight in my heart."* Needless to say, because of the marital counseling he received, he has gone on to be an excellent husband and father. But the "for better or for worse and for richer and for poorer" is real.

Even at my own wedding, reality hit me. While my wife and I were down on our knees praying, I heard the LORD say, *"this is the wife you asked me for,"* and I broke into tears in front of 250 guests. Most of the people thought I was overly excited. But I was thinking, *what in the world did I just do? I just signed up to be a husband and I don't know how to be one.* I remember getting up off my knees, wiping the tears from my eyes, and saying, *my life will never be the same.*

I was right. This journey called marriage has taken me and my wife through each of the vows we made.

IN SICKNESS AND IN HEALTH

As a little boy, I remember asking my grandmother *"Grandma, why do people marry sick people?"* Her reply was *"normally they don't marry sick people, but people get sick sometimes during the course of their marriage."*

Very shortly after being married to my wife, I was diagnosed with ulcerative colitis, a very serious disease of the colon. Not knowing what she had signed up for, it really took my wife by surprise.

Because she loved me, she walked with me through it--and I mean *through it.* My doctor told me that I would have to live with this disease for the rest of my life. *But God.* I said, *but God.*

But God said in Isaiah 53:4-5,

> Surely he took up our pain and bore our suffering, yet we considered him punished by God, stricken by him, and afflicted. But he was pierced for our transgressions, he was crushed for our iniquities; the punishment that brought us peace was on him, and by his wounds we are healed.

God, through His miraculous healing power, healed my body. There is no trace of colitis in my body. Thank God for healing me. I'm 58 years old now and that happened when I was 25 years old. My wife has stuck by my side through every sickness I've ever encountered, from the common cold, car accidents, back problems, double pneumonia, and a host of other unnamed sicknesses. We stuck together through every one of them, and you can, too.

FOR RICHER OR POORER

This vow may be one of the most challenging vows of all. MagnifyMoney's 2017 Divorce and Debt Survey polled a national sample of 500 divorced U.S. adults to understand how money played into the end of their relationship.

Here are the key findings:

AMONG ALL SURVEY RESPONDENTS

More money=more problems

Among all respondents, 21% cited money as the cause of their divorce. The more money a respondent earned, the more likely they were to cite money as the cause of their divorce. Among people who earned $100,000 or more, 33% cited money as the cause of their divorce. By contrast, only 25% of people who earned $50,000 to $99,999 cited money as the cause of their divorce. And the lowest income-earners, those earning $50,000 and under, were the least likely to say money was the cause of their divorce at just 18%.

Money might cause more stress for younger couples. While rates of divorce rose along with a couple's earnings, the opposite seemed to be true when it came to age. Younger couples reported that financial issues drove them to divorce, while the rate went down for older couples. Among 25 to 44-year-olds, 24% cited money as the cause of their divorce. Among 45 to 64-year-olds, 20% cited money as the cause of their divorce. Among those 65 and over, 18% cited money as the cause of their divorce.

We can see that money can be a real problem if we don't handle it right. The bible probably talks about money more than anything else because it's such a necessity in our lives. If we are going to have a successful marriage, we must be a master of our money.

The bible says in Matthews 6:24, ''No one can serve two masters. Either you will hate the one and love the other, or you will be devoted to the one and despise the other. You cannot serve both God and money." God knows we need money to survive here on Earth. He has promised to supply all of our needs according to his riches in glory (Philippians 4:19). God doesn't want us to love money and material things more than we love Him.

The bible says *"the love of money is the root of all evil" (1 Timothy 6:10).* This is one of the most misquoted scriptures in the bible. It doesn't say money is the root of all evil, but *the LOVE* of it. Loving money more than loving the God who created the money can really MESS up our priorities. In fact, the bible says "those who want to get rich fall into temptation and a trap and into many foolish and harmful desires that plunge people into ruin and destruction. For the love of money is a root of all kinds of evil (1 Timothy 6:9-10 NIV)."

Some people, eager for money, have wandered from the faith and pierced themselves with many griefs (v. 10). If we love it more than God Almighty, it will turn our hearts from the LORD and cause us to face many griefs as well. The word "grief" means deep sorrow, misery, sadness, anguish, pain, distress, heartache, heartbreak, agony, torment, affliction, suffering, woe, desolation, dejection, and despair. No wonder it causes so many divorces.

FOR BETTER OR FOR WORSE

I believe it is important to note that every day will not be a day of sunshine in your marriage; there has to be some rain. There is an old saying, "I couldn't appreciate the sunshine if there was no rain. I couldn't appreciate the heat if there was no cold. I couldn't appreciate the summer if there was no winter." Ecclesiastes says, "to everything there is a season and a time to every purpose under the heaven...He hath made everything beautiful in his time" (Ecclesiastes 3:1, 11 KJV).

There will be times when better will become worse, but if you hang on in there and keep loving, keep being responsible for one another, things can get better. Often when I officiate a wedding, I suggest to the bride and groom to incorporate in the wedding ceremony a tradition taken from the Yoruba culture whereby a bride and groom are asked to taste four elements. The couple animates as they taste each item. Ranging from bitter to sweet, these elements are a lemon wedge, vinegar, cayenne pepper, and honey. The reason I ask the bride and groom to incorporate this tradition in their ceremony is to remind them that life will sometimes be bitter, sour, spicy, and sweet.

We must learn how to accept all of these if we're going to enjoy a beautiful and healthy marriage.

If couples understand that life itself brings its share of joy as well as pain, they will be more prepared to deal with the troubles of life.

Not long ago, I took a couple through my one-year counseling course. They enjoyed a beautiful wedding and honeymoon. After enjoying a year together, tragedy struck in their marriage. The husband went out to get his wife her first anniversary gift and was involved in a one-car accident. I was called by his wife to the hospital to pray for him.

The news wasn't good. The husband was diagnosed with a fractured spinal cord. As a result, he was paralyzed from the waist down. This was a catastrophic turn of events from their wedding day. To go from jubilation to devastation is not what they had in mind.

A few years later, the wife came and told me, "if it wasn't for your premarital counseling and teaching us the difference between a covenant and contract, we don't know if we could have survived this calamity." 1 Corinthians 7:28 says, "But if you marry, you have not sinned: and if a virgin marries, she has not sinned. But those who marry will face many troubles in this life, and I want to spare you this" (NIV).

Troubles will accompany marriage. But if you thoroughly prepare yourselves for them, you can truly survive the "for better and for worse" of life.

I can attest to their story because I have my own. After enjoying 29 years of a beautiful marriage, a lovely daughter, a successful business, and a growing church, the better became worse. I had just bought my wife the home of her dreams. She had been supporting me in my dreams as a minister and pastor our entire marriage. I wanted to reward her for always being there, for supporting and encouraging me to do God's will for my life. Then my wife was suddenly laid off from her job. At the same time, the church I pastor was facing a financial crisis.

Never in our 29 years of marriage did we ever face a financial challenge at the same time. I did everything I could as a man to save our dream home, but it was not to be. We were evicted from our home in January 2017. A day I will never forget.

So many marriages failed because of the housing crisis of 2008. There were moments I thought I would be a statistic of that crisis. But on the way to put all of our worldly possessions in storage, with tears covering my face, I made a vow to God that I would not let this awful calamity destroy my family. I made this vow fully knowing what the word says: "It is better not to make a vow than to make one and not fulfill it (Ecclesiastes 5:5 NIV)."

Everything I taught the couples I'd counseled, I, too had to put into practice. Not having any place to go, I had to put my family in an extended stay hotel room for 9 months. To move from a 5,500 square foot house to a 10x10 square foot room was unimaginable. I was faced with two choices: either I could make the best of a bad situation, or quit.

Needless to say, quitting on my family in a time of crisis never crossed my mind. In fact, my wife and I became even closer in our relationship. We never had one argument. We never blamed one another for what had happened. We never stopped caring for each other the whole nine months because we kept God in the center of our lives. We took our vows seriously. We signed up for better and we also signed up for worse.

I never stopped pastoring the people I loved. We didn't miss one church service to the Lord. After the nine months was over, my wife and I did a tag team sermon to let our church know "God will provide," which was our sermon topic.

For all of you who are reading this book, you don't have to let a tragedy determine your life. Your tragedy can become your triumph. Not long after we moved into a rental home, my wife obtained a job that exceeded her goal. My financial situation has changed as well. We are now in a position to buy a new home because we didn't give up on God or one another.

You too can survive the martial vows if you keep your marriage in between the sheets of the Bible. God has a plan if you just allow his word to be a lamp unto you feet and a light unto your path (Psalm 119:105). You can survive the better or for worse.

Acknowledgements

I am indebted to a host of professionals who influenced me to write down my marital counseling experiences in this book. Bishop T.D. Jakes, the late great Dr. Miles Monroe, Professor Dr. Mary Quinn, and an unnumbered amount of people and especially my late father in the ministry Bishop George H. Haskins Jr. I know you are praising the Father God with the angels. I will see you when I get there.

I would like to thank the couples I've counseled over the last 35 years. I have helped couples and individuals get through the challenging times in their marriage. We have cried together as you shared your many disappointments and pain. Your honesty and transparency have allowed this book to come to fruition. I truly appreciate and thank you for allowing me to assist you with the word of God.

To my church family, New Beginning Christian Center. You have challenged me to share the knowledge of marriage with couples around the world. Thank you for allowing me to fulfill another gift from God which is counseling. Your patience and your commitments to New Beginning Christian Center overwhelms me with gladness and appreciation to know that I have a church family that is supportive and willing to stick with me through the fire. I love you and thank you for always being there.

To the great Mothers who God has so graciously blessed me to be impacted by your love.

Mother Mabel Lewis, I thank you for entrusting me with my wife and your daughter. Because of you, my wife has been my rock and the woman of my dreams. Watching you serve the Lord, has impacted both of our lives. You planted a seed long ago and that tree has grown to bear good fruit.

Mother Shirley Matthews, I thank you for passing down the generational blessing of the gift for writing. As I recall your poems, a black mother's lullaby, they will forever be engraved in my heart. I know that this book would have made you a proud mom. This book was written with you in mind. Love you mom.

To my two best friends in the whole world.

Anthony Humphries. 25 years ago, you allowed me to counsel you and your wife. You also allowed me to officiate my first wedding ceremony. Your friendship means a lot to me, brother. It's very rare that one can have a friendship that lasts 40 years, but ours has stood the test of a generation. Thanks, man, for being there.

Mark Osborne. My spiritual brother, you have been to me what Johnathan has been to David for over 40 years also. You are a consistent covenant brother in Christ. You have encouraged me throughout the years to be all that God has created me to be. Thank you for your steadfast love for me and my family. You have welcomed us openly and have always provided us with a home away from home. Mark, we have a track record together and I am so grateful to have you as my brother. Continue to serve the Lord and press towards the mark of the prize of the high calling which is in Christ Jesus. Finish your ministry with JOY!

To my beautiful, amazing, and gifted daughter, Shannon Melvin. From the moment you came into this world, you have captivated my heart. I want you to know that daddy loves you. Always work towards your goals and dreams. Remember we have taught you to be the woman God created you to be. Set a goal and go after it. You can be and do whatever it is that you set your mind to do. Our hope is that you will look into this book one day and let it bless your life and your marriage. Thank you for your patience, understanding, and love. Daddy

To my amazing wife, helpmate and friend, Sheila Melvin. You have given me 37 amazing years of your life. I often jokingly say to you that I have been with you longer than I have been with myself. The years spent with you have been the most rewarding and fulfilling years of my life. Thank you for your continuous support. You have been a constant motivation, encouraging me to finish what I have started. You have been an awesome First Lady to our church and an even more wonderful mother to our daughter. To me, you have been that virtuous woman in Proverbs 31, a God-fearing wife, my best friend, and my irreplaceable rib. I cannot take all of the credit for this project. You have been there to listen to my ideas and provide me with feedback. You have truly been by my side throughout this project. Please know that the time spent away from you to work on this book has allowed me to have a renewed sense of marriage. Since I have found you, I know that I have obtained the favor of the Lord. Sheila, we are one and I will always love you from the bottom of my heart.

Made in the USA
Columbia, SC
15 November 2020